MW01247514

Safia Guerras was moved and inspired to write poetry after attending a Haiku recital, compelling her to express a reckoning with her inner self. She aims to share her inner voice to assist others in overcoming their struggles.

Born in Algeria, Safia's global travels have not only been a source of personal enlightenment but also spurred her creativity, leading her to become a fashion designer, interior designer, writer, and inventor.

For the past two decades, settled in the Middle East to raise her children, she has pondered life's meaning, drawing from her experiences and observations. She writes in English, her third language.

This book introduces Safia, not as a daughter, wife, mother, sister, or friend, but simply as Safia, the human being.

I would like to dedicate this book to my mother and my father.

Safia Hussein Guerras

O.N.E - OPPORTUNITIES NEVER END

AUSTIN MACAULEY PUBLISHERS™

LONDON • CAMBRIDGE • NEW YORK • SHARJAH

A CIP catalogue record for this title is available from the British Library.

ISBN 9781035834723 (Paperback)
ISBN 9781035834730 (Hardback)
ISBN 9781035834754 (ePub e-book)
ISBN 9781035834747 (Audiobook)

www.austinmacauley.com

First Published 2024
Austin Macauley Publishers Ltd®
1 Canada Square
Canary Wharf
London
E14 5AA

"I've learned that people will forget what you said, people will forget what you did but people will never forget how you made them feel" – Maya Angelou

The beginning is yet
To unfold.
Stories start at the end.

Happiness is a choice,
Not a place,
Rather to embrace.

Don't despair,
Life is fair,
If you dare.

Life is a flash
Of light in the
Dark, I hide.

Where to begin
When the end
Is near I fear.

Once upon a time,
We were once One.
Now we've converted into me.
I reached the extremity
Of endless thirst
For the meaning of being.

The curtains that
Separate us have
Exposed the gospel truth.

The soul to the shadow,
The dark in the bright
Daylight I come into sight.

Good and evil
Aren't equal; our
Actions are their distinctions.

Everlasting bliss
Is he who knows less
Is being blessed.

Each soul is a flash of light
That shines only for
A moment of time.

Forgive to heal,
If you want to live,
Reveal the righteous one.

If we embrace our pain
As much as our joy,
Impossible becomes possible.
We are light;
Fading away to darkness
Is our weakness.

Life is worth abides
In the abundant heart of
The one who's satisfied.

The gift of giving is gracious;
It symbolises a gesture,
The souls identify with.

Truth does not hurt or harm;
It only enlightens
The darkness inside.

Love has brought life,
Turned into light, and
Made everything right.

Love is our togetherness
With space in between;
We become oneness.

Love is infinite.
The soul that carries it
Is indeed the dear one.

Love never ends;
Only the ends
Of people's stories.
Love was present;
I was trapped
In my past.

The tragic life story
Is that you are loved
But I was unaware.

Pure love comes from
An unknown place;
It manifests in limited time.

Love has no agenda.
It manifests purely
And fulfils itself.

Love doesn't
Begin or end;
It's an infinite journey.

Love's miracle begins with
Someone you don't even
Know exists.

A child without love
Is a day without light.
Let not the dark envelope his sight.

Injustice has spread
In the hearts that love,
Afflicting endless pain.
To love and to be
Loved are the
Nourishment to the soul.

Pain and love,
Like silky gloves,
Protect the heart.

The heart was hijacked,
Condemned
To endless pain.

Love is as precious
As your own soul;
Both unseen, they exist.

Happiness consists in
The realisation and
Contentment of the moment.

Love, you are
Residing inside you,
Longing to be found.

Love's metamorphoses
Are endless, converting
Time into infinity.

Step wandering,
Turn on mode,
Awakening.

In the contemplation of night
And day, perfectly paired
And balanced we are.

I cried when no one
Was around for long,
And alone, I testify.

Exposed yet composed,
Without a sound, I exploded;
Behind the curtain, I hide.

Born to complete,
Not to compete;
Argue the self and ego.

Once we were brave
To rave with one voice;
Apart we are here and now.

The absence of courage
Has entrapped your wings
To fly through the wind.

The nest was a fortress,
Forced to fly across the sun;
I light upon the guardian wings.

My treasures are internal,
In silence, I keep them
Hidden in the mystic river.

I have changed,
In stages evolving,
From nothing to every little thing.

The realities of life
Aren't letting me
Heal so I can live.

I am lost
In my thoughts,
Banned from my own.

I am alone with you,
And when I am with you,
I am with you alone.

You cease to exist if
Deprived of the five
Miracles of life.

In the treasure of early
Hours, behind the evil I confess
To the hearer of all my grace.
My wonder's in the palm
Of my hand, counting
Till five I sense the divine.

I am innocent of your
Ignorance of Thee;
For faith is one's fate.

The absence of what was missing
Inside me was Thee,
And that brought back light to me.

Decrease the volume
From near and far
To lie with the divine.

The human body
Has become subject,
Turned into an object.

The soul is infinite,
Over and above the
Muddy body.

Love has parted away;
I found Thee
Caring for me.
I have lost my battle
In the west but find myself
In the east closer to Thee.

Faith is the air,
Invisible yet there,
I bear to care.

Be good, do good,
For goodness is the crown
Of greatness.

The odds were against us;
Only Thee
Said, "Be."

Upon reading the sacred
Words, the screen was lifted,
A cloud-like mass to sunrise.

In the duration of time
And its movement, there
Are moments called now.

The day of gathering is
The delight to one,
The dismay of the departing.

Glorifying Thee
At any given time is
The meaning of being.
The present moment
Has faded away,
Faraway from the pathway.

My past and future
Have become an infinite
Scar.

The present light
Is fading gradually
From my sight.

Overtaking the past,
Overwhelming the present,
Overshadowing the future.

In the present time,
Left are my past memories,
Reminding me of an uncertain future.

Past, present,
And future,
Time has passed by.

Time and distance
Are self-remedy
To be.

Every second of life
Is a gift, for the next
Is not granted.
We are infinite beings;
Time is meaningless
In life's limitless journey.

You are of value,
Beautiful one, be bold
To hold onto your gladness.

Blindsided to grasp
The wonders around,
Nowhere to be found.

Currently,
The absence of simplicity
Has shifted into absurdity.

Our relationship with anger
Has caused a destructive
Companionship effect.

Trusting in the judgement
Of the scrutiniser instead
Of your mirror, beautiful one.

Unconscious about
Your inner beauty,
Absorbed by virtual reality.

Your sight has been
Destitute of the vision
Of your own value.
The compassionate heart
Apprehends the affinity
Of brotherly love.

Being compassionate
Means grasping the significance
Of the importance of all.

Truth hurts the ego,
Not the soul that
Lights the heart.

May you find something
Which is not a thing,
For life is being alive.

Goodness is when you
Nurture your nature to
Be kind.

Words are instruments
Of transmission, conveying
Harmony in speech.

You loved my precious
Gift unconditionally
Until I opened it.

Polluted thoughts ruin
The current state of the
Present moment.
I want to ride
Till the end
So I can start again.

Allowing pride and
Ego to guide you
Will kill you.

We are one in
Two different bodies,
Struggling to be.

Struggle, the greatest
Human characteristic
Of survival.

Paired as one,
Light at the end of the dark,
We survived.

Life's importance is
The human
Insignificance.

Lost and found
Are the mysteries
Now and then.

You lied once, then
Twice; which part of you
Are you lying?
When the soul, heart,
And mind are aligned,
A straight path is designed.

Life and death
Made a covenant; the
Soul laughs at both silently.

Our morals are the
Compass to navigate
Life's turbulence.

Wrapped in a veil of anger,
In an invisible
Shape, I fade.

Don't say a word;
The world needs
More than words.

Silent pain and piercing cry,
The grievances of the innocents,
Convey the voice.

Joy and pain made a
Power to balance out
My grief, to believe.

Words have great
Effect; they can
Poison or heal you.
Expectations ruin
The joy out of every
Aspect of life.

The thoughts of the mind
Are reminiscing
The bleeding heart.

Don't play with me;
I am not a game,
But a human with lots of pain.

Pleasing yourself
Is better than losing it
To everyone else.

Don't cheat
Yourself while
You are alive.

Be alive, for
Life is only a
Blink of an eye.

Love and pain are
Bound together inasmuch
As their source starts in the heart.

Human essence
Is fading away
From the meaning
Of being.

I am what I am;
You are what you are;
Let's stop pretending what we are not.

Being alone is not being lonely;
Alone you started,
Alone you will end.

To love and to be
Loved are the
Nourishment to the soul.

Only myself and I
Interpret the fragments
Of my life.

Everything is fading,
Remaining is the presence
Of the One and Only.

Home is not a place
Or someone you
Own, one hope

In a bright daylight
A single smile might
Light someone's sight

In the vast spectrum of
Life, makes one wonder
Of its minor honour

A good life is
To do right
And what is left
You are being blessed

Trapped in a nest of
Yesterday, sadness
For fear of future tears

Love of desires are
Endless appetite in
Starving, suffering world

The gardens beneath which
Rivers flow, I want to go
Hope the patient ones

Each day feels like a page
Of a storybook which tells
The tales of fictional truth

Assumptions are deceptions
Be conscious of their actions
They lead to displease ease

Impact the world with your
Words, to give rise and
Justify what is right

In a world of freedom
Enslaved to addictions
Lost in life's wisdom

Discrimination is a disgrace
To any human race face
Brace the case into grace

Life and death are the
Beginning and end
Of an infinite tale

The bridge that separates
Love from hate, is the
One who breaks it
Our success is inspired
From within the unseen
Attest to its true origin

We have one life, all in all,
Different paths leading
Where's one heading

The bed of sadness
Nurturing its madness
Result in nothingness

You are not alone as
Long as you are
Living, is being

Most are lost to lust
Time turns into dust
Image to mirage

Pain without complain
Choice without a voice
Embrace all with grace

Provided for beforehand
I lend in the hands of my
Mother's land, I give thanks

Longing for desire
Does not appease ease
It distracts the inner peace
Deceived by evil, mislead
By people, leading the human
Being away from the pathway

Don't undermine the gift
Of the present time, it's
Always now to be found

Lovely little light
My path in life was bright
To fight the battle of life

Please and thank you
Are worthwhile words
To lighten the world

The thought of your name
Framed inside, beside
All the pain, I remain fine

Each day, a bit of me is
Lost in the vast yet
Confined mind of mine

Bear witness to the evilness
We share with the wickedness
Unwilling to perceive realness

I am only a human being
Inspired from within
To conceive what is real
Trapped inside a room
Full of boredom rumours
Spread to humour them

Don't despair, the air will
Not remain the same, for
Tears will lead to breeze

In my solitude, away from
Such gatherings, I light upon
A meadow of enlightenment

I longed to reach dreamland
Shores for long, got caught in
Line of the author's clever plot

We have exchanged climate
Change for nowadays trend
To interchange human change

Let your calmness blow
Away the clouds of worry
Into a still stream of ease

The sky isn't the limit
Above and beyond are
Seven leading to heaven

In every home, there is grief
Upon every cheek, are tears
Grief is where love lived
Today's life special
Illusion and delusion
Nutritional solutions

Be thankful in times of
Ease and sorrows, joy and
Pain are heavenly made

Current state of mind
Not to be disturb
Don't mind your mind

Suspended by daydream
Caught in the line of time
To an unchanged change

Actions have impacts
Colliding with different
Paths to endlessness

Oh noble ones who reach
The sky, be careful of the
Numbers of shooting stars

All the perhaps make up
Our comfort, and maybe
Discomfort will bring hope

Be content with what
You have, richness is the
Haunt for a hungry appetite
Sickness doesn't come
From what you eat but
From what is eating you

Through hardship, the greatest
Achievements were made, in
Pain there's gain to be attained

Happiness resides
Inside, not around
Or outside the nest

Life is too short, don't
Make it shorter with
Oblivious predicaments

Be thankful, patient kind
In their regards are the
blessings and rewards

Be not in appearance
happiness doesn't reside
In comfort and wealth

Why does one cry over
Possessions, when I don't
Possess my own soul

Death has no favourites
The mighty or the feeble
Will face the coup de grâce
Depression does not
recognise or stand in awe
Of names wealth or position